40 L
extra
40 ^Bites

A Family Guide to Pray for the World

Trudi Parkes

Population figures for countries are based on the United Nations Population Fund (World Population Dashboard 2022). Figures over ten million have been rounded to the nearest million; countries under ten million have been rounded to the nearest hundred thousand.

This book belongs to

_____

And I am going to pray for the world

Use this guide to pray for the world every day for 40 days or once a week on a special day.

Contents

Tick each day when you've prayed for that country or topic.

Tick each day when you've prayed for that country or topic.

Day 1. Belgium

Population: **12 million**
Main Religion: **Christianity**
Capital: **Brussels**
Official Languages:
Dutch (Flemish), French and German

'I in them and you in me—so that they may be brought to complete unity. Then the world will know that you sent me and have loved them even as you have loved me.' JOHN 17:23 NIV

What do chocolate, waffles, French fries and Tintin have in common?

Yes, you've guessed it! Belgium!

French fries aren't French but are named after French-speaking Belgians who claim they invented them! Tintin is a world-famous Belgian comic series! And Belgians make and sell a lot of waffles and delicious chocolate!

Belgium is a small country in Western Europe between France and the Netherlands. Its capital city, Brussels, is the headquarters of the European Union, and the vegetable, Brussels sprouts, was named after it!

NEW WORD
*Immigrant: a person who has come to live permanently in a different country from the one they were born in.

Belgium is mainly divided between Dutch-speaking Flemings in the north called Flanders, and French-speaking Walloons in the south called Wallonia. Unfortunately, the different languages and cultures of these two main parts of Belgium have meant that there has been disunity.

Many Belgians say they are Catholic, but sadly, few go to church or have a living relationship with Christ. There is also a growing amount of people who are non-religious and don't have a faith at all. Praise God, however, that the number of evangelical Christians is increasing mainly because of the vibrant faith of immigrants* who have moved to live in Belgium. Let's pray that they would be an example of unity and a light to the nation of Belgium, bringing God's peace and drawing many Belgians into a relationship with the Lord.

 **PRAY**

- For unity between the Flemings and Walloons.

- For Belgian believers to be an example of unity and draw others to Christ.

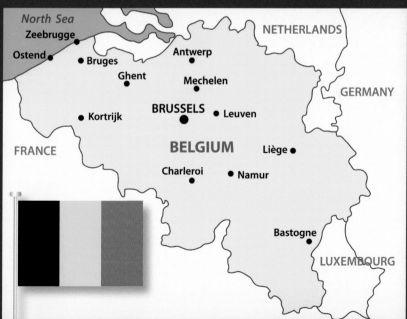

Day 2. Justice

'Speak up for those who cannot speak for themselves. Defend the rights of all those who have nothing. Speak up and judge fairly. Defend the rights of the poor and needy.' PROVERBS 31:8-9

A child cannot go to school just because she's a girl!

A refugee flees from war and poverty but has nowhere to go!

A woman works long hours in a clothing factory in dangerous conditions with little pay, yet the company gets richer!

A man is sent to a labour camp for being a Christian!

A woman is paid less than a man for doing the same job!

A boy is trafficked* to work as a slave making bricks and cannot escape!

A poor family, including their children, work hard growing bananas but only get a tiny part of the final price.

It's not fair! But sadly, the poor and weak are sometimes taken advantage of or treated badly like this! Justice means treating people fairly. God wants us to treat people justly and with love and kindness. The Bible tells us to speak up against injustices when people are being treated unfairly by those who have power or authority over them.

NEW WORD
*Human trafficking: the crime of buying or selling people or making money from work they are forced to do.

 PRAY

● For safety, freedom and help for those who are being treated unfairly.

– 8 –

So, what can we do?

- We can pray for people to be treated fairly and justly.
- We can stand up against injustice by raising awareness about these situations, writing to governments to point them out or by signing petitions.
- We can buy from companies who treat their workers well.
- We can give to the poor so that they are not so vulnerable.

Get into it!

Next time you go shopping, look for food like bananas and chocolate that have a sticker with a Fairtrade logo on. It means that the people who produced them in poorer countries work in safe conditions and get a fair price for their work. This supports the farmers and workers by improving their lives and communities and means many children can go to school rather than having to work.

Day 3. Peru

Population: **34 million**
Main Religion: **Christianity**
Capital: **Lima**
Official Languages:
Spanish, Quechua and Aymara

'Now this is eternal life: that they know you, the only true God, and Jesus Christ, whom you have sent.' JOHN 17:3 NIV

Do you know where the fictional character, Paddington Bear, comes from? Or where potatoes originally come from?

Peru! - a country in South America with beautiful coasts, the Andes Mountains and the Amazon Rainforest. In Peru you can find animals called llamas and alpacas and discover Machu Picchu, an ancient city high up in the mountains built by the Incas. As one of the new seven wonders of the world, this is the most visited place in Peru!

Many Peruvians are poor, so some move to cities to find work but end up living in slums. Sadly, Peru has many street children and has problems with illegal drug production, human trafficking and social injustice of vulnerable people.

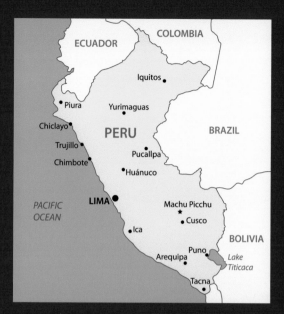

The main religion in Peru is Christianity. Most Christians are Catholic, but many of them practise a combination of Christianity and Paganism*, meaning they also believe in animism and witchcraft. They don't realise that truly knowing Jesus Christ as Saviour and following only him is the best thing we can do with our lives.

Praise God, the number and influence of evangelical Christians in Peru is growing. They are trying to help bring justice and freedom to the poor and vulnerable people, particularly indigenous people* such as the Quechua and Aymara, as well as Amazonian people groups. God is also answering prayers, with Peruvians being set free from Paganism and coming to true faith in Jesus Christ.

PRAY

- That Peruvians would know Jesus as their only true God.

Day 4. Earthquakes

'God is our protection and our strength. He always helps in times of trouble. So we will not be afraid if the earth shakes, or if the mountains fall into the sea.' PSALM 46:1-2

The ground we walk on seems solid, but it is actually made up of huge pieces of flat rock called tectonic plates. These move very, very slowly. Earthquakes are the sudden violent shaking of the Earth's surface and happen when a plate scrapes, bumps or drags along another plate.

Do you know that hundreds of earthquakes occur around the world every day? We don't notice most of them because they are so small.

Occasionally, however, an earthquake can be very powerful and can cause a lot of damage. The average earthquake lasts only

PRAY

● For God's protection and strength for people affected by earthquakes.

10-30 seconds and yet can cause houses and buildings to collapse and people to be injured or even killed. Sometimes the shaking or tremors can be felt thousands of miles away. After an earthquake, electricity and fresh water can be lost, and it can be difficult to get food and basic supplies.

Scientists use numbers from one to ten to describe an earthquake's strength. This number system is called a scale or a magnitude scale. Higher numbers mean stronger earthquakes and often more damage. The largest recorded earthquake happened in Chile in 1960 and was 9.5!

Earthquakes cannot be prevented, but in countries like Japan, where they happen more often, they try to build houses and buildings that are less likely to collapse when there's an earthquake. Unfortunately, poor countries can't afford to do this, and it can take years to rebuild again.

Day 5. Bangladesh

Population: 168 million
Main Religion: Islam
Capital: Dhaka
Official Language: Bengali

'The Spirit of the Lord is in me. This is because God chose me to tell the Good News to the poor.' LUKE 4:18

You may have heard of Bangladesh from reports on the news about its frequent floods or maybe read labels inside clothes in your wardrobe which say, 'Made in Bangladesh'.

'Bangladesh' means 'land of the Bengalis'. It's a country surrounded by India, Myanmar and the Bay of Bengal. It is a beautiful country with long beaches, mangrove* forests, tea plantations and friendly people. Bangladesh is crowded with many people working as farmers or in factories making clothes. Working in clothing factories can involve long, difficult hours, and the women and children who work there earn very little money.

-14-

PRAY

- For Bangladeshi people to hear the good news.

- For Bangladeshi Christians to continue showing God's love despite being treated badly for their faith.

NEW WORDS

*Mangrove: a tropical tree found near water, whose twisted roots grow partly above ground.

*Unreached people group: a people group that has not yet been reached with the gospel.

Unfortunately, Bangladesh also often suffers from flooding because it is a flat, low-lying country with many rivers and heavy rainfall during the monsoon season. Floods and cyclones can cause many people to lose their homes, crops and animals and even cause deaths.

Bangladesh is mainly a Muslim country, but there are also some Hindus. Most Bangladeshis are Bengali, one of the world's largest unreached people groups*. Many of them are yet to hear the good news of Jesus.

There are not many Christians in Bangladesh, and those who have converted from a Muslim background are sometimes treated badly for their faith. Praise God, the church, however, is starting to grow, and the Christian community is trying to help the country, especially the poor, and show them the love of Christ.

Day 6. Ship Ministry

'I pray that the God who gives hope will fill you with much joy and peace while you trust in him.' ROMANS 15:13

Did you know that ships are used to share about Jesus and his love with people around the world? They travel to different countries and places, bringing hope to many and changing lives. The OM ship, *Logos Hope*, shares knowledge, help and hope with people in port cities around the world. It has a huge bookfair, with thousands of educational and Christian books, which local people can visit. The crew give practical help and care in the surrounding communities and share their hope in Jesus with people they meet. Some ships are medical ones, like the Mercy Ships, *Africa Mercy* and *Global Mercy*, which bring free healthcare to poor people in desperate need. Onboard these ships, volunteer surgeons perform free operations and train local medical workers.

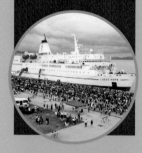

👏 PRAY

- For God to continue using these ships to bring his love, hope, healing and life to people around the world.

- For God to provide the people and money needed to run the ships.

NEW WORD

*Cleft lip and palate: a gap or split in the upper lip and roof of the mouth present at birth.

Meet Baby Junior

Baby Junior had a cleft lip and palate* and so was unable to feed. He weighed only 4.5lb (2kg), was growing weaker and constantly cried for food. His mother feared that he would die and so took him to a medical ship that had just arrived at a port in the African country of Cameroon. The medical staff on the *Africa Mercy* hospital ship fed Junior through a tube to make him strong. He then had two operations that enabled him to eat properly and grow, which changed his life forever. His mum was so relieved and delighted and said, 'The Lord has changed the life of Junior and given him a new one'.

Photo © Mercy Ships

Day 7. Israel

DID YOU KNOW?

Between Israel and Jordan is the Dead Sea which is the lowest point on Earth and has water so salty that you can't sink in it!

Population: **8.9 million**

Main Religion: **Judaism**

Capital: **Jerusalem**
(Although not widely recognised internationally)

Official Language:
Hebrew (Arabic has special status)

'Pray for peace in Jerusalem:
"May those who love her be safe."'
PSALM 122:6

Israel, the Holy Land!

This is how Israel, a small country in the Middle East, is often described. It's because Israel is home to many holy places, the greatest of which is Jerusalem, a special city in Israel, a place that is holy for three major religions: Judaism, Islam and Christianity.

Israel is also sometimes described as the Land of the Bible. It's where Jesus was born, lived and died. Many places you've read about in the Bible, such as Nazareth, Beersheba and the Sea of Galilee, are all in Israel.

Most people in Israel are Jews, and so between sunset Friday evening and sunset Saturday evening, they have their day of rest called the Shabbat. Shops close and work is not allowed.

Israel is an ancient country,

PRAY

- For peace between Palestinian and Jewish people.

- For all people living in Israel to accept Jesus as the true Messiah and their Saviour.

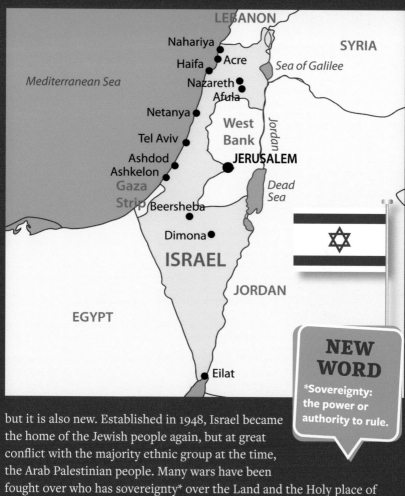

NEW WORD

*Sovereignty: the power or authority to rule.

but it is also new. Established in 1948, Israel became the home of the Jewish people again, but at great conflict with the majority ethnic group at the time, the Arab Palestinian people. Many wars have been fought over who has sovereignty* over the Land and the Holy place of Jerusalem since then. This conflict sadly continues today. Psalm 122 says to pray for the peace of Jerusalem, so let's pray this fighting would end and that there would be *Shalom*, the Hebrew word for peace.

There are not many Christians in Israel but praise God, there is now more interest in the gospel, and the church is growing.

Wouldn't it be amazing to see God, the Holy One of Israel, recognised and worshipped as the Messiah and Saviour of both the Jews and Palestinians in Israel so they can live together peacefully?

Day 8. Child Sponsorship

"'For I know the plans I have for you," declares the LORD, "plans to prosper you and not to harm you, plans to give you hope and a future."' JEREMIAH 29:11 NIV

Have you ever thought about sponsoring a child who is poor? Do you know what child sponsorship is?

Sponsoring a child means giving a small amount of money every month, writing to that child, praying for them and being part of God's plan in their lives. Sponsorship can change the lives of children who are poor, showing them that they matter and giving them hope and a future.

Children who are poor often can't afford to go to school, get help when they are sick or have enough food to eat. Some children end up working to survive, and some may die because their families don't have enough money.

Child sponsorship gave Richmond hope and a future

Meet Richmond

Richmond was a young boy living in Uganda when his father was killed. His family lived in one small room with a leaking roof. They didn't have enough food to eat, and Richmond couldn't go to school.

Poverty made Richmond feel hopeless and that he didn't matter to anyone. Then one day, he received the news that a 15-year-old girl called Heather had decided to sponsor him. Richmond says he doesn't have the words to describe the joy that filled his home the day he was told he had a sponsor and so could go to school again. Letters from Heather and her prayers gave him hope, and when he was older, Richmond gave his life to Jesus and now works as a pastor.

PRAY

- For more poor children to be sponsored.

- For sponsored children to experience hope and a future in Jesus.

Day 9. Azerbaijan

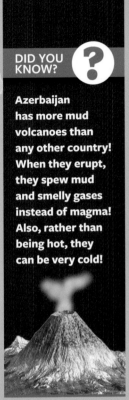

Population: **10 million**
Main Religion: **Islam**
Capital: **Baku**
Official Language: **Azerbaijani**

'They said to each other, "When Jesus talked to us on the road, it felt like a fire burning in us. It was exciting when he explained the true meaning of the Scriptures."' LUKE 24:32

Azerbaijan, the Land of Fire!

A country where tea is drunk through lumps of sugar or jam held in the mouth and where Chovgan, its national sport and a game similar to polo, is played to music!

Azerbaijan is famous for weaving carpets, mud volcanoes and its chess championships! Every year people visit its wall of fire on a mountain that's been burning for over 65 years! The flames don't go out because of the natural gases that seep from the ground.

Azerbaijan is a country in both Europe and Asia surrounded by Russia, Georgia, Iran, Armenia and the Caspian Sea. It was part of the former Soviet Union for many years but has been independent since 1991. Unfortunately, since then, there has been on-and-off conflict and fighting over land between Azerbaijan and Armenia.

Most people in Azerbaijan are Muslim and although not many know Jesus, the church in Azerbaijan is growing, especially in the capital city. Many towns and villages, however, have never heard the gospel. Let's pray they would hear about Jesus and, as they do, that they would feel 'fire burning in their hearts' compelling them to faith in Christ.

PRAY

- For Azerbaijanis in the towns and villages to hear the gospel and follow Jesus.

- For no further conflict over land with neighbouring Armenia.

Day 10. Sports Ministry

Football coaching for children left vulnerable by poverty.

'All those who compete in the games use strict training. They do this so that they can win a crown. That crown is an earthly thing that lasts only a short time. But our crown will continue forever.' 1 CORINTHIANS 9:25

Here's a question for you! Ready, Steady, Go!

What do Bukayo Saka, an Arsenal football player, Alisson Becker, a Liverpool goalkeeper and Nicola McDermott, an Olympic high jumper, have in common?

Yes, you're right! They are all Christians who play sport!

Do you like playing sport? What's your favourite sport to watch or play?

Being involved in sports can be a way to share the love of Jesus with others. It could be through Christians in sport telling other competitors, players or fans about their faith. Or using sporting events such as the World Cup or

Golf balls were originally made from dried cow eyeballs, and strings on tennis rackets used to be made with sheep intestines! Grass at Wimbledon was kept two inches (5cm) long until 1949, when a snake bit an English tennis player!

the Olympics to share the gospel. Or through coaching, competitions or camps for children and young people to help them improve their sport while also hearing about Christianity.

Meet Wanchai

Wanchai leads a Compassion project for children at a church in Chiang Mai, Thailand. Most of the children live in the slums and are poor. Their parents often work late in the evenings, so the children, especially the boys, roam the streets with nothing to do. The project started football coaching for the boys every Saturday and Sunday. Now the boys are so tired from the football that they stay at home and sleep instead. This has meant that they are safer and less vulnerable to child trafficking. Some of the boys have also come to believe in Jesus.

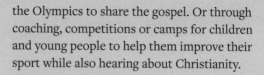

PRAY

- For opportunities in sport to share the gospel with others.

Day 11. Sudan

Population: **46 million**
Main Religion: **Islam**
Capital: **Khartoum**
Official Languages:
Arabic and English

'*...fixing our eyes on Jesus, the pioneer and perfecter of faith.*' HEBREWS 12:2 NIV

'I am determined to continue trusting the Lord, even if things are uncertain!' said Seida, whose husband was killed for his faith in Sudan.

Seida grew up as a Muslim in Sudan and left Islam to follow Christ. After the death of her husband, she fled to the Nuba Mountains. Her family are trying to persuade her to stop being a Christian and return to Islam again, but despite her difficulties, she is keeping her eyes fixed on Jesus and remaining strong in her faith.

Praise God for the faith and trust of Sudanese Christians as they face persecution for their faith in Christ.

Sudan is a country in north-eastern Africa that used to be the largest African country by land size. After many years of unrest and fighting between a mainly Arab Muslim north and a mainly African Christian south, it eventually split, and the south formed the newest country in the

world called South Sudan. Sudan is now the third largest country in Africa.

Sudan is mainly Muslim. Sadly, Christian Sudanese people like Seida are often treated badly for simply believing in Jesus.

It used to be against the law and punishable by death for a Muslim to become a Christian but praise God, this has now changed, which is an answer to the prayers of many Christians. Let's continue to pray for Sudan - for the Christians who are being persecuted and for many Sudanese to turn to Jesus.

PRAY

- Praise God for the faith and trust of Sudanese Christians in God.

- For freedom, strength and protection of Christians in Sudan.

- For Sudanese Muslims to come to faith in Christ.

Day 12. Animism

'Where God's love is, there is no fear, because God's perfect love takes away fear.'
1 JOHN 4:18

Animism is the belief that all things, such as plants, animals, rocks and thunder, have spirits in them. These spirits and gods are unpredictable and can help or harm people. Animists, therefore, try to influence the spirits by worshipping them or trying to appease them through offerings, sacrifices and prayers. Some animists will also make offerings to their dead relatives hoping that the spirits of their ancestors will bring them good fortune.

Animists believe that witch doctors, medicine men and shamans* understand the spirit world. They go to them for help and protection.

Animism can be found in many tribal or ancient religions. Some people also mix animistic beliefs and practices with major religions like Islam, Hinduism, Buddhism and even Christianity.

NEW WORD

*Shaman: a religious leader and healer of the sick who is believed to have special powers.

PRAY

- For the fear that animists experience to be replaced with God's love and peace.

- For more people to share about Jesus with unreached tribes, who are animists.

Worshipping spirits and witchcraft is not pleasing to God, and he warns against them in the Bible. Animists live in fear of the spirit world, but we praise God that Jesus holds all power and authority, and we can know peace and freedom if we trust in him.

Meet Daw Tin May

Daw Tin May lived in a constant state of fear. She worried that she might anger the spirits and bring harm to her family. To appease the spirits, she offered sacrifices of animals and food. One night she was invited to a Christmas celebration at a church near her village in a Southeast Asian country. She went and watched the Jesus film§ and heard about Jesus, the sacrificial Lamb of God who died on the cross to save us and who has power over evil spirits. She broke down in tears and gave her life to God!

§ *The Jesus film is a movie about the life of Jesus Christ, translated into over 1,900 different languages.*

A spirit house used to worship or appease spirits.

Day 13. Canada

Population: **38 million**
Main Religion: **Christianity**
Capital: **Ottawa**
Official Languages:
             English and French

'May he rule from sea to sea and from the River to the ends of the earth.'
PSALM 72:8 NIV

The second largest country in the world by land area! Home to the most lakes in the world! Almost half of the country covered in forest!

Maple syrup, ice hockey, grizzly bears and beavers! This is Canada!

Canada is a huge country to the north of the United States. It extends from the Atlantic to the Pacific and northward into the Arctic Ocean. Compared to its size, it has quite a small population of about 38 million people.

Canada is a country that has welcomed immigrants and so now over a fifth of the people are from other countries. This means that society is a mixture of languages, cultures and religions.

Canada has Christian history, and many people in Canada are Christians. Sadly, however, the number of Christians and people attending church has decreased in recent years.

The Canadian national motto is 'From Sea to Sea' and comes from Psalm 72:8. Let's pray for all people in Canada, across the whole country, from sea to sea, whether they are French-speaking or English-speaking, immigrants from other countries or indigenous people, such as the First

Nations, Métis and Inuit. Let's pray that they will know God and want to share about him with other people.

Get into it!

Look at the Canadian flag with the symbol of a maple leaf on it. Maple syrup is made from the sap of sugar maple, red maple and black maple trees grown in Canada!

Try pouring it over waffles and then enjoy eating it while praying for Canada.

🖐 PRAY

- That the Canadian church would be a witness to God, drawing people to him.

- That Canada would bring glory to God from sea to sea across its vast country and to other countries.

Day 14. Adoption and Fostering

'A father to the fatherless, a defender of widows, is God in his holy dwelling. God sets the lonely in families.' PSALM 68:5-6 NIV

Have you or any of your family or friends been adopted or fostered?

Did you know that in the Bible, Moses, a great and godly leader, was adopted by an Egyptian princess? And that Samuel, a prophet of God, was fostered by Eli?

God sees adoption and fostering as very important! At least 40 times, the Bible refers to God's concern for orphans or the fatherless! That's more than the number of times it talks about tithing or taking communion!

 **PRAY**

- For more people to adopt and foster.
- For fostered or adopted children to experience God's love and healing.

Adoption is permanently and legally bringing up another child as your own when the birth family is unable to do so or when the child is not safe. Fostering is caring for a child for a short or long time, sometimes until the child's parents can look after them again or while they are waiting to be adopted.

These children deserve homes where they can be loved, valued and thrive, whether in foster care or with a new adoptive family.

Meet Kayla

Kayla and her brother were fostered when they were three and five years old because their mum was addicted to drugs and was neglecting them. Now they live with a foster family where they have settled and are starting to thrive again.

What can we do?

Be a church that welcomes and supports people adopting and fostering? Pray and support charities such as Home for Good or World Without Orphans, which are trying to find homes for all children who need one, especially older children and siblings? Or maybe even be part of a family God has called to adopt or foster?

Day 15. Laos

Population: 7.5 million
Main Religion: Buddhism
Capital: Vientiane
Official Language: Lao

'Tell the nations about the Lord's glory.
Tell all peoples about his wonderful works.'
1 CHRONICLES 16:24

Have you ever heard of the country called Laos? It is a beautiful country mainly covered in mountains with thick green forests. The islands on the mighty Mekong River, which flows through Laos, are stunning. Laos is the only landlocked country in South East Asia and is one of just a few communist countries* in the world today.

Many Laotians live in the countryside and are very poor. About half of them are ethnic Lao people, but the rest of the population is made up of over a hundred different people groups, many of whom have yet to hear the gospel.

Buddhism, mixed with animism or spirit worship, is the main religion. There are only a

PRAY

- That all the tribes and people groups in Laos would have the opportunity to hear the good news.

- For perseverance and courage of believers in Laos when faced with persecution.

small number of Christians. Christianity is not against the law, but it is seen as a foreign religion and a threat. Believers are, therefore, sometimes treated badly for their faith. Praise God, despite this, the church is growing, and people are turning to God.

Prai tribe

A Prai man living in a remote mountain village in Laos was given an SD card inside a little speaker with the gospel message on it. He hid it under his pillow and secretly listened to the good news every night. After a while, he responded by giving his life to the Lord. Praise God! Through his faith, others in his family and village have also come to Jesus.

Day 16. Sikhism

'I myself am the Lord. I am the only Saviour.' ISAIAH 43:11

Do you know anyone living near you who is a Sikh? They can sometimes be identified by the turbans that the men wear to cover their uncut hair.

Over 20 million people follow Sikhism, making it the sixth-largest religion in the world. Sikhs live in many countries but mainly in the Punjab area of India.

The religion was started over 500 years ago by Guru Nanak, the first of ten gurus who were the leaders of the faith. Their teachings are written in the holy book called the Guru Granth Sahib.

Sikhs worship in a temple called a Gurdwara. When Sikhs enter the Gurdwara, they cover their heads and take off their shoes. There aren't any

The five physical symbols of faith worn by committed Sikhs are called the five Ks.

- **Kesh** - uncut hair

- **Kara** - a steel bracelet

- **Kanga** - a wooden comb

- **Kaccha** - cotton underwear

- **Kirpan** - a steel sword

🙏 PRAY

- For the gospel to reach every Sikh.

chairs inside, so people sit on the floor. After the service, they eat food together.

Sikhs believe in one God and emphasize doing good rather than rituals. They believe that after death, we are reborn into a new body and that good or bad actions in this life affect the next life. To become united with God and end this cycle, Sikhs try to live their lives by working hard, being honest, treating everyone equally, sharing and helping others and keeping God in their hearts and minds.

Jesus loves Sikhs, and he wants them to know him. Let's pray that Sikhs would put their faith in Jesus Christ, the only way to God, and the only one who forgives, saves and gives new life.

Gurdwara Bangla Sahib in New Delhi, India, is instantly recognisable by its golden dome.

Day 17. Malta

Population: **0.4 million**
Main Religion: **Christianity**
Capital: **Valletta**
Official Languages:
Maltese and English

'When we were safe on land, we learned that the island was called Malta... The people on the island gave us many honours. We stayed there three months.'
ACTS 28:1 & 10

Malta is an island country located in the Mediterranean Sea. It's an archipelago, meaning it's a group of islands, of which Malta is the largest. Although Malta is one of the world's smallest countries at just 17 miles (27km) long and 8 miles (13km) wide, it's a fascinating country with lots of interesting history. Many tourists enjoy its warm climate, historical monuments, rocky cliffs, and its stunning coasts with clear blue sea and white sand. There are five times more tourists visiting the island every year than there are residents!

Malta is a religious country, with most Maltese being Roman Catholic. It has only one Maltese university and yet has 365 Catholic churches! That's one for every day of

🙏 PRAY

- For the Maltese to have a personal living relationship with Christ.

- For the migrants and refugees from North Africa to hear the good news of Jesus.

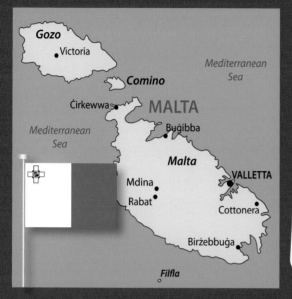

the year! It holds many celebrations and feasts throughout the year in honour of the patron saints*. Malta is even mentioned in the Bible! In Acts 28, we read that Paul landed there after being shipwrecked and that he brought Christianity to the island. He spent three months there, and many miracles were seen. Sadly, despite all this, not many Maltese have a personal relationship with the Lord Jesus. Let's pray they would experience the joy of having a living faith in Christ.

Malta also receives Muslim refugees and migrants* arriving by boat, mainly from nearby North Africa. They also need to hear the good news of Jesus.

The magnificent fortress city of Valletta, capital of Malta.

Day 18. Business as Mission

A fish farm in Bangladesh

'In the same way, you should be a light for other people. Live so that they will see the good things you do. Live so that they will praise your Father in heaven.' MATTHEW 5:16

Business as mission is a way of using a business to share the good news of Christ with people who have never heard the gospel before. It can be an opportunity to show care to its workers and be an example of God's love.

The business could be anything from a coffee shop to a language school. It could be a factory that makes clothes in Nepal, an IT company in Romania, a fish farm in Bangladesh, a fitness company in Jordan, an ice-cream factory in Central Asia or farming in Mozambique.

It may be in a country which only allows missionaries to live and work if they have a business. Or it may be in a poor place where creating jobs helps

PRAY

- For more business people to use their gifts and skills for God's glory, especially among the world's poorest and least-reached people.

- For businesses to be used to help people and share the gospel.

DID YOU KNOW?

The average person will spend over 13 years of their life at work! Workplaces are important places with huge opportunities to share the good news!

families and communities and helps prevent poverty, human trafficking and injustices.

Meet Raimund

A German Christian businessman opened a factory in a poor, rural village in northern Thailand, making deodorants out of alum crystals. This really helped families and the community and provided a safe, enjoyable workplace for many people. At the beginning of each day, Raimund encouraged his workers to join a short meeting where he shared about Jesus. Over time, more and more workers attended the meeting, some came to faith in Christ, and a small church began.

Day 19. United Arab Emirates

Population: **10 million**
Main Religion: **Islam**
Capital: **Abu Dhabi city**
Official Language: **Arabic**

'Then they will know that you are the Lord. They will know that only you are God Most High over all the earth.' Psalm 83:18

PRAY

- For opportunities for Christians to share the gospel wisely with unbelievers.

- For Emiratis to come to faith in Jesus Christ.

This country is no stranger to the Guinness World Records! It loves breaking world records for having the biggest and best of certain things. It has the world's tallest building, the largest Ferris wheel, the fastest rollercoaster and the deepest swimming pool!

The United Arab Emirates is a modern, hot, desert country between Saudi Arabia and Oman in the Arabian Peninsula*. It's also called the Emirates or

NEW WORD

* Peninsula: an area of land surrounded by water on three sides.

the UAE and is made up of seven emirates (states), including Dubai, each with its own king (sheikh).

It used to be a country that was poor and dependent on fishing, but over 50 years ago it discovered oil, making it a richer and more developed country.

Only about 11% of people living in the UAE are local Emiratis; the rest are foreign workers from other countries. Although the UAE is mainly Muslim, it is tolerant of other cultures and religions and allows Christians to meet to worship God. It is, however, illegal to share about Jesus with Muslim Emiratis or for them to become Christians.

Praise God, some foreign workers who are Christian are sharing their faith with others in the UAE, and some people are deciding to follow Jesus. There are still, however, few Emirati Christians.

We know that Jesus is the best and highest above all things – let's pray that the Emiratis and foreign workers who don't know Jesus will also know this and give their lives to him.

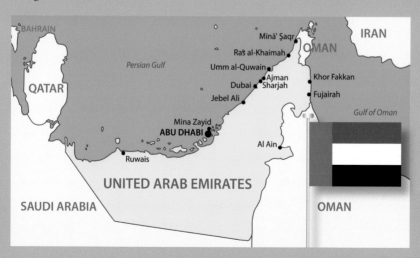

Day 20. Mekong River

'There is a river which brings joy to the city of God.'
PSALM 46:4

The Mekong River is the longest river in South East Asia. It is about 2,700 miles (4,350km) long and flows from China, along the borders of Myanmar, Thailand, Laos and through Cambodia and Vietnam.

The people who live along the Mekong River use the river for transport and to fish and grow crops, particularly rice. Dams built on the river are used for hydroelectric power, and in Vietnam, the river is used for floating markets where people sell things from their boats. There's a photo of a floating market on the next page.

NEW WORD

* Taoism: a Chinese way of life that teaches people to lead a simple life in harmony with nature.

Of the 60 million people who live by the river, there are many unreached people groups, each with their own language, culture and religion. Sadly, many have never heard the gospel before.

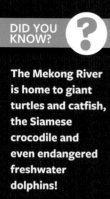

PRAY

- That as the river flows and moves through six countries, God would move in the lives of people who live close to the Mekong River with many coming to know God.

- For more workers to share the good news of Jesus.

Mien

The Mien are a people group who live in the mountains in southern China, Vietnam, Laos and Thailand, close to the Mekong River. Most of them have beliefs in animism and Taoism*, and only a few are Christian.

One Mien man listened to a Mien Christian radio programme and heard that God can help people leave the worship of spirits. Spirit worship was terrible to him because whenever he or his family were sick, he had to call a shaman to do spirit worship. The shaman required him to kill ducks or dogs in order to be healed. All this killing seemed senseless and made him very sad. Praise God, he decided to believe in Jesus and was able to leave spirit worship behind. He began a relationship with God and then had peace in his heart.

Day 21. Morocco

Population: 38 million

Main Religion: Islam

Capital: Rabat

Official Languages: Arabic and Berber

'The Son of Man came to find lost people and save them.' LUKE 19:10

Morocco is an Arab country in North Africa. A strip of water called the Straits of Gibraltar separates it from Europe by just eight miles! Every year millions of tourists enjoy Morocco's beautiful beaches, colourful towns, ornate mosques and interesting markets along narrow streets. They even visit the Sahara Desert.

They taste mint tea served with sugar, fine wheat pasta called couscous and tagine, a slow-cooked stew, which takes its name from the clay dish it's cooked in.

The two main people groups in Morocco are Arabs and Berbers, and religion is a very important part of their lives. Morocco is 99% Muslim, and Moroccans are encouraged to pray five times a day and fast during the month of Ramadan. They are proud that they live in an Islamic country.

Sadly, there are very few Moroccan Christians, and many have never heard the gospel. It is difficult to share the good news in Morocco, and having an Arabic Bible is against the law.

Moroccans are expected to be loyal to Islam, king and country. If a Muslim decides to follow Jesus, life can often be hard for them. They may be

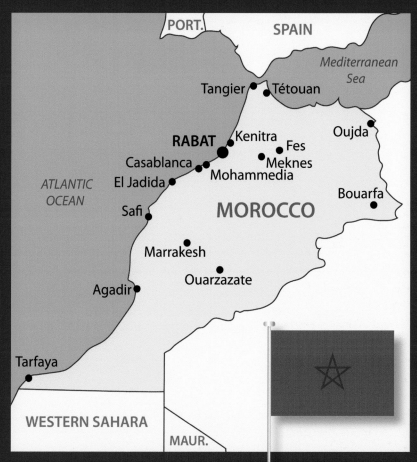

accused of being disloyal and bringing shame to their family and community. Some may be treated badly because of their faith, and many find it difficult to meet with other believers.

We thank God that Jesus came to save the lost and that he wants to save Moroccans. Let's pray that many Moroccans hear the gospel and come to faith in Christ.

🫲 PRAY

- For Moroccan Arabs and Berbers to hear the gospel.

- For new Christians to grow in their faith and be able to meet safely with other believers.

Day 22. Bible Literacy

'All Scripture is given by God and is useful for teaching and for showing people what is wrong in their lives.' 2 TIMOTHY 3:16

More than one in ten people around the world are unable to read this sentence, let alone this book! To be illiterate means that you are not able to read or write. Can you imagine being unable to read a book or a newspaper, read labels on medicine bottles, write your name or send a message to a friend! Life would be very difficult.

In some areas of the world, millions of children who are poor will never go to school, and they will never learn to read or write.

The Bible is one of the most read books in the world, but sadly, some people cannot read it and learn more about Jesus. Illiteracy can also stop Christians from sharing the gospel.

PRAY

- For Christians to be able to read the Bible and so grow in their faith.

- For unbelievers to decide to follow Jesus as they learn to read and write and discover the Bible.

Meet Angelique

Angelique is a girl from the Central African Republic. There was a church in her village, but her parents didn't let her go to it because they were animists. However, they did let her go to lessons to read and write taught by the pastor because this was the only school in the village. She learnt how to read, memorise Bible verses and pray. At home she would repeat the verses in front of her family until her parents began to go to church, where they then gave their lives to Jesus! Since becoming followers of Jesus, Angelique's family has changed. She says, 'We can now read, write and count little by little. Thank you, God!

Day 23. Fiji

Population: **0.9 million**
Main Religion: **Christianity**
Capital: **Suva**
Official Languages:
English, iTaukei (Fijian) and Fiji Hindi

NEW WORD

* Cyclone: a violent tropical storm with very strong winds (formed over the South Pacific and Indian Ocean).

'I beg that all of you agree with each other, so that you will not be divided into groups.'
1 CORINTHIANS 1:10

Climate problems, such as global warming and rising sea levels, threaten Fiji!

The country of Fiji is a group of about 330 islands in the South Pacific Ocean east of Australia, of which about 100 are inhabited. These islands are small and low-lying, so rising sea levels cause areas to flood, making it

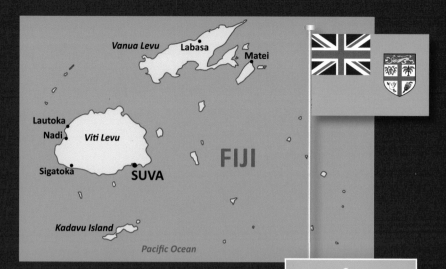

hard to grow crops. Global warming means Fiji also experiences more frequent and intense cyclones*, and the warmer seas are damaging its coral reefs.

Despite these problems, Fiji is still often described as a tropical paradise with its turquoise blue sea and beaches lined with palm trees. It attracts many tourists who enjoy riding in canoes to explore islands and snorkelling to see coral reefs and colourful fish.

Over half the people in Fiji are native Fijians (iTaukei), and about a third are Indian Fijians. Over a hundred years ago, when the British used to rule Fiji, many people were brought from India to work in the sugar cane fields in Fiji. Sadly, Indian Fijians and native Fijians have resented each other, and there has been continued conflict between them.

We thank God that many Fijians are Christian, and some have even gone to other countries as missionaries. Not many Indian Fijians, however, are followers of Jesus; most are Hindu or Muslim. Let's pray the relationship between native Fijians and Indian Fijians would heal and that Indian Fijians would be reached with the gospel.

PRAY

- That native Fijians and Indian Fijians would live at peace with one another.

- For Indian Fijians to hear the good news and accept Jesus as their Saviour.

Day 24. Arab World

'After this, I will give
my Spirit freely to all
kinds of people. Your
sons and daughters will
prophesy. Your old men
will dream dreams.
Your young men will
see visions.' JOEL 2:28

PRAY

- For Arab Muslims to have dreams
  and visions in which they meet Jesus.

- For Arabs to come to faith in the one
  and true God.

The Arab world is the area
of the world where there are Arabic-speaking countries and populations. It
consists of 22 countries in Africa and Asia which are members of the Arab
League. Over 420 million people live in the Arab world, and most of them
are Muslims.

What do you imagine when you think of Arabs? Men wearing long white
robes and a headdress held in place by a black band? Women wearing long

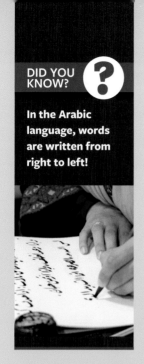

black cloaks with a headscarf called the hijab and sometimes a face cover called the burka? These are the traditional clothes of some Arabs. Have you ever heard Arab Muslims greet each other? They say 'As-salamu Alaikum', which means 'Peace be upon you'.

In the Arab world, many unreached people groups are yet to hear the gospel. God is, however, moving by his Spirit and drawing people to himself. One way he is revealing himself to people is through dreams.

Meet Hamid

Thirty-two-year-old Hamid awoke with his heart pounding. Such a strange dream! What did it mean? Hamid dreamt he was being buried in sand, and someone rescued him by taking hold of his hand and pulling him out of the sandy pit. The rescuer was a man shining with light who said, 'I have paid the full price for you. Rest and follow Me.' After this dream, Hamid decided to find out about Christianity and eventually put his faith in Jesus, the light of the world.

Get into it!

Buy some Arabic food such as pita bread and hummus from your supermarket. Tear the pita bread into pieces and dip them in the hummus. Just before you eat it, pray for Arab people to become Christians.

Day 25. Singapore

Population: **5.9 million**
Main Religion: **Buddhism**
Capital: **Singapore**
Official Languages:
Mandarin, English, Malay and Tamil

'But seek first his kingdom and his righteousness, and all these things will be given to you as well.' MATTHEW 6:33 NIV

MALAYSIA

Sembawang
Woodlands
Nee Soon
Ubin
Tekong Besar
Choa Chu Kang
Serangoon
Ang Mo Kio
Jurong
SINGAPORE
Tuas
Bedok
Queenstown
Telok Blangah
Jurong
Sentosa
Sudong
Bukum
Singapore strait
Pawai
Semakau

Singapore is a city, a state and a country! It's a tiny island in South East Asia that you could drive across in just one hour!

Although it is small, it attracts many tourists who enjoy tasting its national dish (Hainanese chicken rice), viewing its statue and national symbol (the Merlion) and admiring Marina Bay Sands (a building with a boat-like roof). They even love visiting its airport containing a rainforest and the world's tallest indoor waterfall!

PRAY

- Thank God for Singapore believers sharing the gospel in Singapore and other countries.

- For more Singaporeans to know Jesus and to seek after him.

Singapore is known as one of the cleanest and greenest cities in the world. Its nature park, 'Gardens by the Bay', contains over 1.5 million plants, with some arranged on structures called 'Supertrees', which thrive in Singapore's hot, humid climate.

There are different religions, languages and cultures in Singapore, yet people live together with respect for one another. Almost all Singaporeans are bilingual, meaning they speak English and another home language such as Mandarin, Malay or Tamil. Over a third of Singaporeans are Buddhist; the rest are Christian, Muslim, Taoist, Hindu or have no religion.

Praise God for the many Singapore Christians who glorify God and for the church, which continues to grow and send out missionaries.

Singapore is one of the richest countries in Asia and has been blessed with unity, freedom and success. Let's pray that Singaporeans would recognise God's blessings on their country and not seek after wealth or achievement but only after the most important thing in life... God!

Day 26. Rohingya

Living conditions in Balukhali camp, Cox's Bazar, Bangladesh, 2017.

'He was hated and rejected by people. He had much pain and suffering.' ISAIAH 53:3

A people without a country or a home! Called the most persecuted minority group in the world! Now living in the world's largest refugee camp!

The situation of the Rohingya refugees has shocked the world.

The Rohingya are a people group who lived in Rakhine State of Myanmar for many years. The Myanmar government said that they were illegal immigrants and wouldn't let them be citizens of Myanmar anymore. They, therefore, couldn't see a doctor when they were sick or even go to school. Then in 2017, violence broke out in Rakhine State, with Rohingya villages being set on fire and Rohingya people being killed. Hundreds of thousands fled for their lives. They walked for miles to join other Rohingya refugees already in nearby Bangladesh. They are now living in a refugee camp, surviving in very basic conditions. Some Rohingya are still left in Myanmar, trapped in camps with little help.

DID YOU KNOW?

Like other people from Myanmar, Rohingya women, children and sometimes men often have patterns of powdery yellow-gold paint on their cheeks and foreheads! This is called thanaka and is made from the bark of a tree. It's used as make-up to keep the skin cool and to prevent sunburn!

PRAY

- For an end to the violence and persecution of the Rohingya.

- For comfort and healing from all they have experienced and lost.

- A place for them to live in peace.

- For Rohingya people to hear about Jesus.

Meet Barkoosam

Barkoosam is 13 years old and lives in the camp in Bangladesh. His father was killed, and he had to flee with his mother and two brothers. He walks for 20 minutes through fields and mud every day to wait in line for food.

Like the Rohingya, Jesus suffered and was also rejected by many. He understands their pain and wants to comfort them and show them his love. Most of them are Muslim, but there are a few Christians.

A Rohingya refugee camp

Day 27. Australia

Kangaroos are born just one inch (2.5cm) long, which is the size of a grape, and there are more kangaroos in Australia than people!

Population: **26 million**
Main Religion: **Christianity**
Capital: **Canberra**
Official Language: **English**

'If you ask me for anything in my name, I will do it.' JOHN 14:14

When some people think of Australia, they think of koala bears and kangaroos because these animals live in the wild only in Australia!

Australia is the sixth largest country in the world by land area and is 32 times bigger than the UK! It is a dry country and often suffers terrible droughts and bushfires. Large areas of the country are called the outback and include deserts that are very hot and dry. Most Australians live near the coast, close to Australia's thousands of lovely beaches. The warm weather and lots of space mean that many Australians love sports such as swimming, surfing, cricket and rugby.

Australia is multicultural, with almost 30% of Australians being born in other countries such as England, India, China, the Philippines and Vietnam. Disappointingly, the number of Christians in Australia has been decreasing, and the number of people with a different religion or no religion at all has been increasing.

God says that if we ask anything in his name, he will do it. Let's pray for a move of the Holy Spirit so

PRAY

- For boldness and wisdom for the Australian church as it shares about Jesus with people of different faiths and cultures.

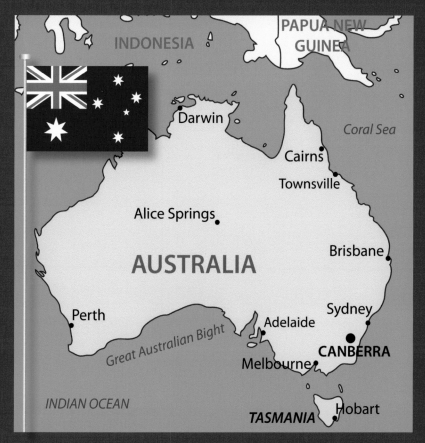

that many Australians, including its migrants and indigenous people, called Aboriginal and Torres Strait Islander people, would come to faith in Christ.

Get into it!

Have you ever played with a boomerang? They are curved flat pieces of wood that can be thrown so that they will return to the thrower! Aboriginal people used them as hunting weapons. Draw and colour in a boomerang. Then stick it on your fridge and use it to remember to pray for Australia.

Day 28. Disability

'Go at once... Bring in the poor, the crippled, the blind, and the lame... I want my house to be full!'
LUKE 14:21 & 23

Did you know that 253 million people in the world are blind or visually impaired? Or that 70 million people are deaf?

Many people in the world have a disability or sickness. Disability is found across all nationalities, races and people and affects one in seven people globally!

For some people, disability can affect their lives, making it difficult to care for themselves or get a job. Sadly, some disabilities are due to poverty and could have been prevented.

THANK YOU

Get into it!

Learn to say 'thank you' in British and American Sign Language!

Flat hand starts with fingertips on the chin. Hand moves down and away from the person signing.

PRAY

- For people with disabilities to feel whole through how they are treated by people and through a relationship with Jesus.

- For more resources to be available, for example, Braille and audio Bibles in more languages.

God has a heart of love and compassion for the sick and disabled and wants to have a relationship with them. He wants them to be valued, loved and supported rather than neglected, forgotten, excluded and treated unequally.

Churches have a role by being welcoming communities for those with disabilities and removing any barriers to them being involved. They can learn how to help, ensure churches and their buildings are accessible and use any resources available, such as having someone interpret a church service into sign language.

Meet Noi

A Christian charity working with a local church in Thailand delivered a children's wheelchair to seven-year-old Noi. Noi's family couldn't afford one, so they were delighted! Now Noi has a way to move around, and the family has started going to the local church where they receive love and support from Christians. Noi's mum said that she believes the wheelchair was a gift from God because it has given them hope!

Day 29. Nigeria

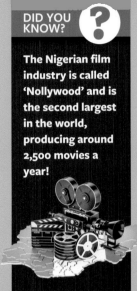

Population: 217 million
Main Religion:
Christianity and Islam
Capital: Abuja
Official Language: English

'There will be no more violence in your country. It will not be ruined or destroyed. You will name your walls Salvation. And you will name your gates Praise.' ISAIAH 60:18

Nigeria is a country in West Africa named after the River Niger, Africa's third largest river. With 217 million people living there, it's the most populated country in Africa and the sixth most populated in the world! It is sometimes called the 'Giant of Africa' because of its large population and economy.

 **PRAY**

- For peace in Nigeria.

- For the protection of persecuted Christians and for them to respond with forgiveness, not retaliation.

- For all Nigerians, from the north to the south, from east to west, to praise the Lord Jesus Christ.

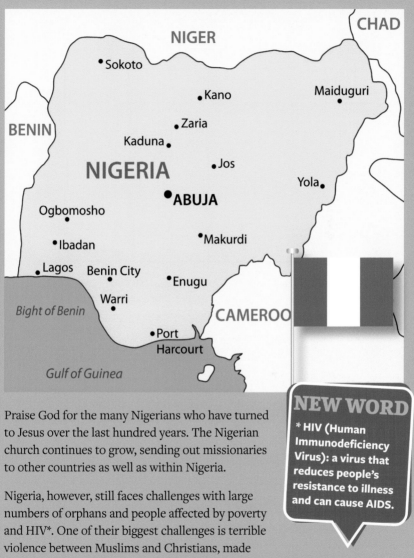

Praise God for the many Nigerians who have turned to Jesus over the last hundred years. The Nigerian church continues to grow, sending out missionaries to other countries as well as within Nigeria.

Nigeria, however, still faces challenges with large numbers of orphans and people affected by poverty and HIV*. One of their biggest challenges is terrible violence between Muslims and Christians, made worse by conflict between different ethnic groups and tribes. Nigeria is divided roughly in half between Christians who live mainly in the south of the country and Muslims who live mainly in the north. Christians living in the north or the middle of the country are particularly persecuted for their faith. Some of their churches have been burnt down, houses destroyed, and many have lost their jobs and even their lives for being Christian.

Day 30. Bedouin

'Let the people of the desert bow down to him.' PSALM 72:9

You are welcomed by a group of people into a tent made of goat's hair on the edge of the desert and offered Arabic coffee, tea and dates. Camels are outside the tent.

Who are these people? They wear ankle-length robes with a headdress and herd camels, goats and sheep.

They are Bedouins which means 'desert dwellers' in Arabic. This group of Arab people live in desert areas in North Africa and the Middle East. In the past, they were nomadic, which means they moved around from place to place and lived in tents.

Today, however, some Bedouins have now settled and live in villages.

Bedouin tribes are Muslim, and so it is hard for Bedouins to become Christians because their families and communities may reject them.

 **PRAY**

- For Bedouin families and communities to come to know Jesus.
- For more people to share about Jesus with Bedouins.

They are so welcoming to guests, often inviting them into their tents to eat and drink, but they are reluctant to show the same openness to Jesus, who is standing at the door wanting to come into their lives. Let's pray that they would open the door to Jesus and then follow and worship him.

Storytelling

John, a missionary, works with Bedouin tribes as a vet for their camels. Camels are so important to Bedouin people because they use them for transport and for their meat and milk. Bedouins love to tell stories, especially through songs and poetry. John, therefore, uses his opportunity as a vet to tell Bedouin people stories from the Bible, including the greatest story of all, Jesus Christ the Saviour.

Day 31. Czechia (Czech Republic)

DID YOU KNOW?

Prague Castle in Czechia is the largest ancient castle in the world! It covers an area the size of 7 football fields and has 4 churches, 4 palaces and over 700 rooms! There's a picture of the castle below and on the next page.

Population: **11 million**
Main Religion: **Non-religious**
Capital: **Prague**
Official Language: **Czech**

'The devil who rules this world has blinded the minds of those who do not believe. They cannot see the light of the Good News—the Good News about the glory of Christ, who is exactly like God.' 2 CORINTHIANS 4:4

If you love castles, medieval towns, spas and beautiful views of forests, rivers and mountains, Czechia (Czech Republic) is the country to visit!

The Czech Republic is a country in Central Europe that has been split up and divided many times. After World War One, the country of Czechoslovakia was formed from the Czech and Slovak lands of the Austria-Hungary Empire. During World War Two, Czechoslovakia became part of Germany, and then after the war, it was under the influence of the Soviet Union and communism until 1990. In 1993, Czechoslovakia separated into two countries: the Czech Republic and Slovakia. A few years ago, the Czech Republic began using Czechia as its official shortened name.

 **PRAY**

- For Czechs to see the light of the good news and decide to follow Jesus.

Czechia is a beautiful country and is now blessed with peace and freedom. It is, however, one of the least religious countries in the world, with over 70% saying they are non-religious. Many do not believe in God or have any religion or faith. Sadly, they cannot see the light of the gospel of Jesus Christ. God's desire is for all Czechs to be saved and to experience the love of God, so let's pray for this country and its people, who are so precious to God.

Day 32. Racism

DID YOU KNOW? ❓

Premier League football players in the UK wear 'No room for racism' badges on their shirts to show unity against racism.

'Now, in Christ, there is no difference between Jew and Greek. There is no difference between slaves and free men. There is no difference between male and female. You are all the same in Christ Jesus.' GALATIANS 3:28

Meet Aisha

At school some children said hurtful things to Aisha just because she was black. It made her want to change the way she looked. One day, she even tried scrubbing her skin, hoping it would change to white. She hated the way others looked down on her. Their words made her feel so bad about herself. Aisha didn't talk to her family about how she felt because they were also struggling. Her older brother was often stopped by the police when he went to the local shop to buy milk!

Have you ever experienced racism?

Racism is when people are treated badly, unfairly or unequally because of their skin colour, language, religion, culture or nationality. It can take the form of words or actions.

God tells us that all people are made in his image and are precious to him. In the Bible, we read about Jesus confronting racism, showing kindness and acceptance to people of all races and treating them equally.

So how should we respond? We need to treat all people equally and with love. We also need to oppose racism and prejudice of any kind. This might be by signing petitions, joining protests or standing up against those who make racist comments.

PRAY

- For all people to be treated equally.

- That God would help us to recognise racism and respond like Jesus.

- For those who have experienced the hurt and pain of racism to experience God's love and healing and know how precious they are.

Get into it!

Can you remember the story of the Good Samaritan in the Bible? We can read it in Luke 10:25-37. The Jews religiously and racially despised the Samaritans in Jesus' day, but Jesus treated Samaritans as equals. He even made a Samaritan the hero in the famous story of the Good Samaritan.

Day 33. Philippines

Population: **113 million**
Main Religion: **Christianity**
Capital: **Manila**
Official Languages:
Filipino and English

'I have made you a light for the non-Jewish nations. You will show people all over the world the way to be saved.' Acts 13:47

The Philippines is an island country in South East Asia named after King Philip II of Spain. It's made up of over 7,000 islands along the Pacific Ring of Fire, an area which experiences a lot of earthquakes and volcanic eruptions. The Philippines also suffers from many typhoons*.

PRAY

- That every Filipino would worship God alone and have a personal relationship with him.

- For Filipino Christians to be a light for Christ all over the world.

Even though over a hundred languages are spoken throughout the Philippines, most Filipinos speak English, making it the fifth-largest English-speaking country in the world.

Sadly, the Philippines has a big gap between the rich and the poor. In cities such as Manila, there are many slum areas and street kids. Many Filipinos try to escape poverty by finding work in other countries as domestic servants, nurses, nannies, teachers or sailors and sending money home to their families. This, however, means that their children are often left behind with relatives and grow up not seeing their parents for years.

Praise God! The Philippines has the fifth-largest Christian population in the world. Most Filipinos have Christian beliefs, with many of them being Roman Catholic. Sadly, some mix witchcraft and animism with Christianity, not worshipping God alone or having a personal relationship with Jesus. We thank God, however, that the evangelical Christian church in the Philippines is growing and sending missionaries around the world. There is also a big opportunity for Filipinos working in other countries to be a light for God.

NEW WORD

* Typhoon: a violent tropical storm with very strong winds (formed over the North West Pacific Ocean).

Day 34. Africa

'At that time you will say, "Praise the Lord, and worship him. Tell everyone what he has done. Tell them how great he is."'
ISAIAH 12:4

Africa is the hottest continent in the world and has the largest hot desert (the Sahara). It is home to the world's tallest animal (giraffe), the largest land mammal (elephant) and the fastest land animal (cheetah).

It is the second largest continent by both size and population. Containing 54 countries, it is home to about 1.3 billion people speaking around 2,000 languages.

Sadly, Africa is the world's poorest and most underdeveloped continent. It has high rates of malaria and HIV, and some Africans are unable to read or write. There is poor sanitation, with many not having access to clean water or a toilet. Also, in some areas, there is fighting and conflict, which makes poverty worse.

 **PRAY**

- Thank God for the many Christians in Africa and those sharing about Jesus with others.
- For unreached people groups and Muslims in North Africa to hear the good news.
- For problems in Africa, such as poverty, fighting and diseases.

Praise God, however, that Christianity has grown hugely in Africa over the last hundred years. Now it is the religion of almost half the people living there. Thank God many of these Christians want to share about Jesus, and how great he is with other Africans and people in other countries.

However, there is still a need for many unreached people groups in Africa, and especially Muslims in the north of the continent, to hear the good news. Let's pray that nothing stops Christians from telling them about Jesus Christ.

Day 35. Turkmenistan

Population: **6.2 million**
Main Religion: **Islam**
Capital: **Ashgabat**
Official Language: **Turkmen**

'All I want is to know Christ and the power of his rising from death.' PHILIPPIANS 3:10

Have you heard of Turkmenistan before? It's one of seven countries in Central Asia with the suffix 'stan' in its name! 'Stan', in ancient Persian, means 'country', and so Turkmenistan means 'country of Turkmen'! It was part of the Soviet Union but became independent in 1991.

🙌 PRAY

- For church leaders and those who have converted from Islam to be strengthened by God when they face persecution.
- For Turkmen to want to know Jesus Christ.

Turkmenistan is 80% desert, and although it's a landlocked country, it borders the Caspian Sea, the world's largest inland body of water, and larger in size than Germany! Turkmenistan is famous for traditional carpet making, its fast Akhal-Teke horses, camels in its Karakum Desert and even a huge fire pit called the Darvaza Gas Crater! The pit was apparently set on fire to burn excess gas quickly, but it still burns today – 50 years later!

Most Turkmen are Muslim, and the Christian church is small. Sadly, many Christians in Turkmenistan are persecuted, especially leaders of churches and those who have converted from Islam.

Meet Pastor Ilmurad

Pastor Ilmurad from Turkmenistan was sentenced to prison for his faith. He had to do hard labour and sleep on a concrete floor. Ilmurad was told that he would be released if he denied his Christian faith, but he refused. Praise God, he was eventually released, and he was thankful for all the support and prayers of Christians around the world.

We thank God that despite persecution, the church continues to grow in Turkmenistan. Let's pray for its leaders as they share the gospel and for Turkmen to hear the good news and want to know Christ.

Day 36. Elderly

'Even when you are old, I will take care of you. Even when your hair has turned grey, I will take care of you... I will carry you, and I will save you.' Isaiah 46:4

Meet Valerie

Valerie is an 83-year-old widow living in the UK. She lives by herself. Her family visit her when they can, but they live far away. Valerie sits at home watching television for many hours each day. She feels lonely at times. One day, someone from her local church visited and invited her to their lunch club for the elderly. Valerie really enjoys the club where she plays games, sings and has heard about Jesus for the first time.

Meet Asafu

Asafu is 78 years old and lives in Ethiopia. She cares for her three grandchildren because their dad left home and their mum is sick. Asafu's family is very poor. She works at a cotton mill but struggles because she has cataracts and needs an eye operation. A charity has supported her through a local church so that she could have the operation, and it has also paid school fees for the children. Asafu is so thankful for their help and love and is interested in knowing more about Jesus.

Two very different elderly women! But both valued and precious.

🙌 PRAY

- For old people who don't know Jesus to come to faith in him.

- For help and strength for the elderly.

The number of old people throughout the world is increasing. Many of them have never heard about Jesus, but it is not too late for them to have the opportunity to come to faith in Christ. Many are also vulnerable, lonely, struggling with health problems, and needing help and care.

Get into it!

Choose one elderly person who you know. Visit them, help them if needed and pray for them.

Day 37. Mauritius

Population: **1.3 million**
Main Religion: **Hinduism**
Capital: **Port Louis**
Official Language (of the National Assembly): **English**

'All I want is to know Christ and the power of his rising from death.' PHILIPPIANS 3:10

An island country created by underwater volcanic eruptions many years ago! That's Mauritius!

Located off the south-east coast of Africa in the Indian Ocean, Mauritius is surrounded by a large coral reef.

Its main island is only about 28 miles (45km) wide and 40 miles (64km) long, yet it attracts thousands of tourists every year. They enjoy its beautiful forests, mountains, white, sandy beaches and lagoons. Tourism and sugar cane plantations have helped make Mauritius one of Africa's more developed and richer countries.

Mauritius was named by Dutch settlers after Prince Maurice van Nassau. As well as the Dutch, the French and the British also occupied Mauritius, but in 1968 it became an independent country.

Many years ago, slaves from other parts of Africa and then later, labourers from India and traders

🙏 PRAY

- For wisdom and boldness for Christian Mauritians as they share the gospel.

- For Mauritian Hindus and Muslims to want to know Christ as their Saviour.

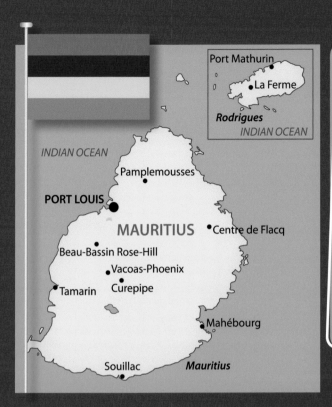

NEW WORDS

* Creole people: people who have African and French or Spanish ancestors.

* Creole language: a language based on French and uses words from African languages.

Port Mathurin
La Ferme
Rodrigues
INDIAN OCEAN

INDIAN OCEAN
Pamplemousses
PORT LOUIS
MAURITIUS
Centre de Flacq
Beau-Bassin Rose-Hill
Vacoas-Phoenix
Tamarin   Curepipe
Mahébourg
Souillac   Mauritius

from China came to live and work in Mauritius. Mauritius is, therefore, a mixture of different races, cultures and languages. About two-thirds of Mauritians are of Indian or Pakistani origin, and the rest are mainly Creole*, Chinese and French. Most people speak Creole*, but some speak Bhojpuri, French or English. The country also has a mixture of religions, but Hinduism is the largest with almost half the population being Hindu.

Sometimes it is difficult to share the gospel in Mauritius because life is very influenced by Hinduism. Praise God, however, that Mauritians, including Hindus, are coming to faith, and the church is growing.

Day 38. Mental Health

'The Lord is close to the broken-hearted. He saves those whose spirits have been crushed.' PSALM 34:18

Mental health is about how we feel, think and act. It's common to feel stressed, frightened or sad at times, and usually, these feelings pass. Sometimes, however, they don't and can develop into mental health disorders like anxiety and depression. Anxiety is having feelings of worry and fear that don't go away. Depression is when you feel sad for a long time and lose interest in doing things you usually enjoy.

Mental ill health can affect anyone, from young and old, rich and famous, to friends and family members.

Looking after our mental health is important, just like taking care of our bodies and being physically healthy. For example, talking and

NEW WORD
* Geocaching: the activity of using GPS to search outdoors for small hidden prizes.

PRAY

- For people with mental health disorders to receive the love, support and help they need.

- That they would know the hope of the gospel and experience God bringing help and comfort.

sharing how we feel with someone, doing fun or relaxing activities and getting enough sleep are all things that help our mental health.

Mental illness is far more common than people think, with about one in five people experiencing mental health disorders, such as anxiety, depression, obsessive-compulsive disorder, bipolar disorder and post-traumatic stress disorder. These people may need medicine and therapy to help them, but they also need support from the people around them. Sadly, sometimes people with mental ill health don't get the support and help they need. Some don't ask for help because they feel embarrassed. In some countries, they may even be treated badly.

Meet Kerry

Shortly after finishing university, Kerry started to experience anxious thoughts, a racing heart, feeling unable to cope with the demands of her new job and occasional panic attacks. She struggled in silence for a few years but then eventually received help and support and felt more positive.

Day 39. Kosovo

Population: **1.8 million**
Main Religion: **Islam**
Capital: **Pristina**
Official Languages:
Albanian and Serbian

'So the churches became stronger in the faith and grew larger every day.' ACTS 16:5

The second youngest country in the world!

Kosovo is a small country in south-eastern Europe that used to be part of the country of Yugoslavia.

In the early 1990s, Yugoslavia broke up after a long power struggle and civil war between different groups. Some of its areas (called republics) became independent countries. Conflict and fighting, however, began between the republic of Serbia and Kosovo (a province within Serbia). Serbia mainly consisted of Serbian Christians, whereas Kosovo consisted mainly of Albanian Muslims. The conflict lasted many years and included the terrible Kosovo War of 1998-1999. Eventually, Kosovo declared itself an independent country in 2008. Many countries recognised its independence, but some countries, including Serbia, still don't recognise Kosovo as an independent country.

The name Kosovo means 'field of blackbirds'. It's a country with beautiful mountains, ski resorts and picturesque towns and villages.

 **PRAY**

- Healing of the relationship between Serbs and Albanians.

- The young church of Kosovo to grow, and its new believers to be strong in their faith.

SERBIA

MONTENEGRO

Mitrovica
Podujevo

Istok

Peć
PRISTINA

Deçan
KOSOVO

Gjilan

Gjakova
Orahovac

Prizren

ALBANIA

NORTH MACEDONIA

*Night view of a crossroad
in the capital of Pristina.*

Unfortunately, it suffered a lot during the conflict and war, with thousands of Kosovans being killed and over a million fleeing the country for safety. It is now one of the poorest countries in Europe with many unemployed people.

Although about 95% of Kosovans are Muslim, there are a growing number of Christian believers. Let's pray that the faith of these new believers will be strong and that the young church will grow as it shares the good news of Jesus Christ with Muslim Kosovans.

Day 40. World Leaders

UNITED NATIONS 🌐 NATIONS UNIES

'You should pray for kings and for all who have authority. Pray for the leaders so that we can have quiet and peaceful lives—lives full of worship and respect for God. This is good, and it pleases God our Saviour.' 1 TIMOTHY 2:2-3

NEW WORDS

* **UNEP:** United Nations Environment Programme

* **WHO:** World Health Organisation

* **UNICEF:** United Nations Children's Fund.

The Bible tells us several times to pray for leaders and those with authority. This includes leaders of our countries, such as prime ministers, presidents, politicians, kings and queens. These leaders may lead well with peace and justice. Or sadly, they may be corrupt and treat some people in their country unfairly or unequally. They may be leaders we didn't choose or don't agree with about issues important to us. God tells us, however, to pray for them all. They all need God's help and to know Jesus as their Saviour.

PRAY

- For leaders to know Jesus and be guided by him.
- For leaders to have wisdom when making decisions and positively impact our communities, countries and the world.
- For those leading unfairly or unkindly to change or be removed from power.

It's also good to pray for leaders of world organisations such as the United Nations, which includes 193 countries. It's called the UN for short. Let's pray they will be united as they work together to keep world peace and make the world a better place. Also, pray for leaders of the UN's various agencies and programmes which try to deal with important global issues, such as climate change (UNEP*), health (WHO*) and children's rights (UNICEF*).

We may never know what impact our prayers may have, but we do know that God is at work in the world and that he is our hope in the middle of any difficult global problems.

Get into it!

Make **W**ednesday the day to pray for **W**orld leaders! Collect pictures or names of various world leaders and put them in a jar. Every Wednesday, pick one out of the jar and pray for them.

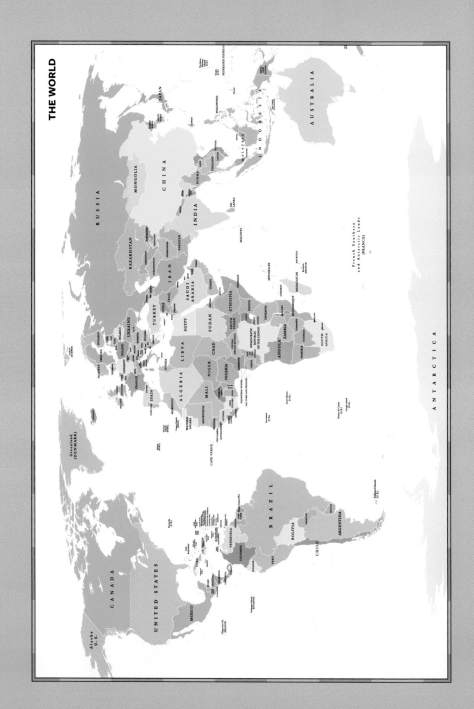

THE WORLD

EUROPE

Greenland
(DENMARK)

ICELAND

Faroe Islands
(DENMARK)

FINLAND

RUSSIA

NORWAY

SWEDEN

ESTONIA

LATVIA

LITHU...

RUSSIA

DENMARK

BELARUS

IRELAND

UNITED
KINGDOM

NETHERLANDS

GERMANY

POLAND

BELGIUM

LUXEMBOURG

UKRAINE

CZECH
REPUBLIC

SLOVAKIA

MOLDOVA

FRANCE

SWITZERLAND

AUSTRIA

HUNGARY

ROMANIA

LIECHTENSTEIN

SLOVENIA

CROATIA

MONACO

BOSNIA
AND
HERZEGOVINA

SERBIA

BULGARIA

ANDORRA

ITALY

SAN MARINO

MONTENEGRO

KOSOVO

MACEDONIA

ALBANIA

TURKEY

PORTUGAL

SPAIN

VATICAN CITY

GREECE

CYPRUS

MALTA

AFRICA

MOROCCO

TUNISIA

WESTERN
SAHARA

ALGERIA

LIBYA

EGYPT

CAPE
VERDE

MAURITANIA

MALI

NIGER

CHAD

SUDAN

ERITREA

SENEGAL

THE GAMBIA

GUINEA-BISSAU

GUINEA

BURKINA
FASO

DJIBOUTI

SIERRA LEONE

CÔTE
D'IVOIRE

GHANA

TOGO

BENIN

NIGERIA

SOUTH
SUDAN

ETHIOPIA

LIBERIA

CENTRAL AFRICAN
REPUBLIC

CAMEROON

SOMALIA

EQUATORIAL
GUINEA

SÃO TOMÉ
AND
PRINCIPE

GABON

REP. OF THE
CONGO

DEMOCRATIC
REPUBLIC
OF THE CONGO

UGANDA

KENYA

RWANDA

BURUNDI

TANZANIA

SEYCHELLES

ANGOLA
(Cabinda)

ANGOLA

ZAMBIA

MOZAMBIQUE

COMOROS

MADAGASCAR

MAURITIUS

ZIMBABWE

NAMIBIA

BOTSWANA

SWAZILAND

SOUTH
AFRICA

LESOTHO

– 87 –

The 40 Days 40 Bites Series

40 Days 40 Bites

This is a book that demands to be read and used in our ministry of prayer for the nations... I will be making use of this prayer guide in my own prayer ministry. Let's work hard together to get this guide out and to get people to really make use of it.
Dr George Verwer, Founder OM

This book covers over 20 different countries including Algeria, China and North Korea. It also includes a variety of issues such as poverty, clean water and translation.

40 Days 40 More Bites

What a brilliant new resource to help families pray for the nations and engage with God's great mission to the world. Every prayer room should have a copy of this book!
Pete Grieg, Co-Founder 24-7 Prayer, Senior Pastor Emmaus Rd, Ambassador Tearfund

This second book in the 40 Days 40 Bites series covers another 20 different countries including Egypt, Madagascar and Afghanistan. It also includes a variety of topics such as orphans, hunger and homelessness.

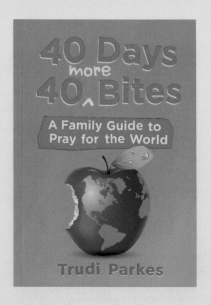

We are an international church-planting movement taking the good news of Jesus to the nations!

Our passion
Loving Jesus- heart and soul, in deed and word

Our mission
Crossing cultures to make disciples
Starting churches where there are none or few
Sharing the vision of the whole church, to the whole world
Praying to see Jesus known, loved and worshipped

Our values
Being devoted to Christ
Relying on him
Denying ourselves to follow him
Serving together in love

UK website: wec-uk.org • International website: wecinternational.org
Email hello@wec-uk.org • Facebook @WECUK • Instagram wecuk

Thank you

I would like to thank the following organisations for giving me permission to use their material:

Mercy Ships for kind permission to use their material for Ship Ministry (Day 6).

OM for kind permission to use their material for Ship Ministry (Day 6).

Compassion International and Richmond Wandera for kind permission to use their testimonies for Child Sponsorship (Day 8).

Compassion International for kind permission to use their testimony for Sports Ministry (Day 10).

Open Doors for kind permission to use their material as a source of information for Sudan (Day 11) and Turkmenistan (Day 35).

Raimund Homberg for kind permission to use his story for Business as Mission (Day 18)

OMF for kind permission to use their material for Mekong River (Day 20).

One Mission Society for kind permission to use their material for Bible Literacy (Day 22).

Arab World Media for kind permission to use their material for Arab World (Day 24).

Tearfund for kind permission to use their material for Rohingya (Day 26).

Image Credits

Front cover and page 2 - Lucie Drobna/Shutterstock.com

Page 9 Justice – 196466048/Thinglass/Shutterstock.com

Page 12 Earthquakes – 106298051/4.murat/Shutterstock.com

Page 16 Ship Ministry - Used by permission of OM

Page 17 Ship Ministry – Used by permission of Mercy Ships

Page 21 Child Sponsorship - Picture on page 21 used by permission of Compassion International, Inc. Copyright © 2020 by Compassion International, Inc. All rights reserved.

Page 24 Sports Ministry - Picture on page 24 used by permission of Compassion International, Inc. Copyright © 2017 by Compassion International, Inc. All rights reserved.

Page 29 Animism – 776342632/NeagoneFo/Shutterstock.com

Page 33 Adoption & Fostering – 752728837/SewCream/Shutterstock.com

Page 36 Sikhism – 1242261589/Matt Hahnewald/Shutterstock.com

Page 40 Business as Mission – 140904457/Stephen Bures/Shutterstock.com

Page 44 Mekong River – 315039404/saiko3p/shutterstock.com

Page 49 Bible Literacy - Used by permission of One Mission Society

Page 52 Arab World – 297418424/michaeljung/Shutterstock.com

Page 56 Rohingya - Living conditions in Balukhali camp, Cox's Bazar, Bangladesh, 2017, Andrew Philip/Tearfund

Page 60 Disability - 1684665043/oxtav/Shutterstock.com

Page 64 Bedouin – 1008275758/Peter Wollinga/Shutterstock.com

Page 69 Racism – 1270777789/TheVisualsYouNeed/Shutterstock.com

Page 72 Africa – 1007424421/RiccardoMayer/Shutterstock.com

Page 76 Elderly - 189903107/Sura Nualpradid/Shutterstock.com

Page 81 Mental Health – 1240892836/SpeedKingz/Shutterstock.com

Page 84 World Leaders – 1193208634/nexus 7/Shutterstock.com

Maps on all country pages - pavalena/123RF.com